EXPLORING ENERGY TECHNOLOGY

SOLAR POWER

EDITED BY ELIZABETH LACHNER

I0809765

Britannica Educational Publishing
IN ASSOCIATION WITH
ROSEN
EDUCATIONAL SERVICES

Published in 2019 by Britannica Educational Publishing (a trademark of Encyclopædia Britannica, Inc.) in association with The Rosen Publishing Group, Inc.
29 East 21st Street, New York, NY 10010

Copyright © 2019 by Encyclopædia Britannica, Inc. Britannica, Encyclopædia Britannica, and the Thistle logo are registered trademarks of Encyclopædia Britannica, Inc. All rights reserved.

Rosen Publishing materials copyright © 2019 The Rosen Publishing Group, Inc. All rights reserved.

Distributed exclusively by Rosen Publishing.
To see additional Britannica Educational Publishing titles, go to rosenpublishing.com.

First Edition

Britannica Educational Publishing
J.E. Luebering: Executive Director, Core Editorial
Andrea R. Field: Managing Editor, Compton's by Britannica

Rosen Publishing
Amelie von Zumbusch: Editor
Brian Garvey: Series Designer/Book Layout
Cindy Reiman: Photography Manager
Nicole DiMella: Photo Researcher

Library of Congress Cataloging-in-Publication Data

Names: Lachner, Elizabeth, editor.
Title: Solar power / edited by Elizabeth Lachner.
Description: New York : Britannica Educational Publishing, in Association with Rosen Educational Services, 2019. | Series: Exploring energy technology | Includes bibliographical references and index. | Audience: Grades 5–8.
Identifiers: LCCN 2018010038| ISBN 9781508106227 (library bound) | ISBN 9781508106210 (pbk.)
Subjects: LCSH: Solar energy—Juvenile literature.
Classification: LCC TJ810.3 .S6265 2019 | DDC 621.47—dc23
LC record available at https://lccn.loc.gov/2018010038

Manufactured in the United States of America

Photo credits: Cover chinaface/E+/Getty Images; cover, back cover and interior pages (background) © iStockphoto.com/tolokonov; pp. 4-5 Kelly vanDellen/Shutterstock.com; p. 7 Yanik Chauvin/Shutterstock.com; p. 9 sumroeng chinnapan/Shutterstock.com; pp. 10, 27 NASA; pp. 12, 14, 24, 31 © Encyclopædia Britannica, Inc.; p. 16 Fadel Senna/AFP/Getty Images; p. 17 Beautiful landscape/Shutterstock.com; p. 20 Vibe Images/Fotolia; p. 22 Smileus/Shutterstock.com; p. 25 Arina P Habich/Shutterstock.com; p. 29 leungchopan/Shutterstock.com; p. 33 Federico Rostagno/Shutterstock.com; p. 35 © Mark Rasmussen/Fotolia; p. 37 RoschetzkyIstockPhoto/iStock/Thinkstock; p. 39 GaryKavanagh/iStock/Thinkstock; p. 40 Antonio Guillem/Shutterstock.com.

CONTENTS

INTRODUCTION

All life on Earth depends on energy from the sun. Solar energy is the source of energy for photosynthesis. It provides the warmth necessary for plants and animals to survive. The heat from the sun causes water on the Earth's surface to evaporate and form clouds that eventually provide fresh rainwater.

Solar energy is the result of thermonuclear fusion reactions deep within the sun. These reactions produce so much energy that they keep the surface temperature of the sun at about 10,300 degrees Fahrenheit (5,700 degrees Celsius). Even though solar energy is the largest source of energy received by the Earth, its intensity at the Earth's surface is actually very low due to the large distance between the Earth and the sun and the fact that the Earth's atmosphere absorbs and scatters some of the radiation. Even on a clear day with the sun directly overhead, the energy that

Solar energy is light, heat, and other forms of energy given off by the sun. Solar energy can be collected and used to heat buildings and to make electricity.

reaches the Earth's surface is reduced about 30 percent by the atmosphere. When the sun is near the horizon and the sky is overcast, the solar energy at ground level can be negligible. It also varies from one point to another on the Earth's surface.

A number of devices for collecting solar energy and converting it into usable energy have been developed. These include concentrating collectors, flat-plate collectors, and photovoltaic cells. Concentrating collectors use the sun's heat to make electricity. A concentrating collector has mirrors that focus large amounts of solar energy into a small area. A flat-plate collector is a large plate of black metal covered with a sheet of glass. It is usually placed on the roof of a building. The plate absorbs sunlight and uses it to heat air or water that flows through pipes behind it. The air or water then goes through the building's heating or plumbing system.

Photovoltaic cells—also called solar cells—use the sun's light rather than its heat. When the sun shines on a solar cell, the cell turns the light energy into electricity. A single solar cell makes only a little electricity. However, groups of solar cells can provide electricity for whole buildings.

Because the intensity of the sun's radiation at the surface of the Earth is so low, collectors designed to capture solar energy must be large in area. Even in sunny parts of the world's temperate regions, for instance, a collector must have a surface area of about 430 square feet (40 square meters) to gather enough energy to serve the energy needs of one person.

Nevertheless, the total amount of solar energy incident on Earth is vastly in excess of the world's

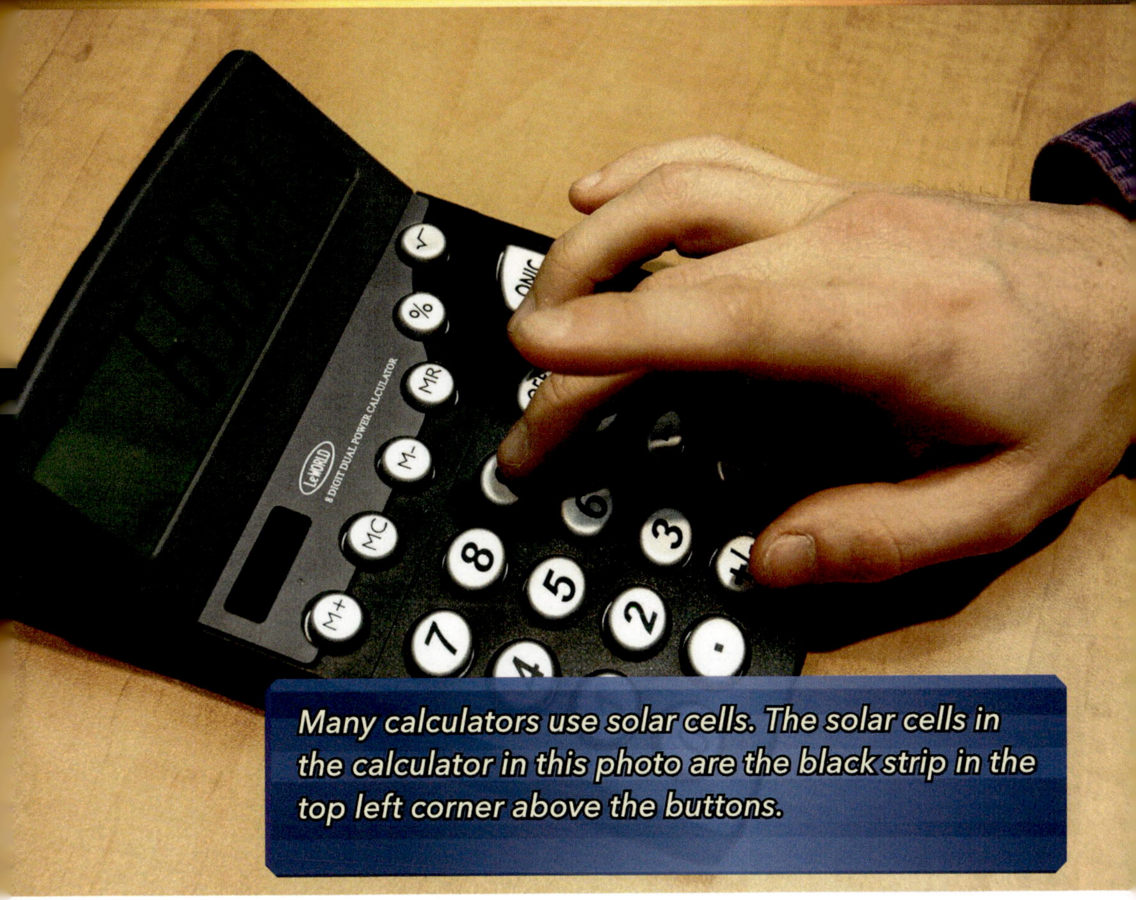

Many calculators use solar cells. The solar cells in the calculator in this photo are the black strip in the top left corner above the buttons.

current and anticipated energy requirements. If suitably harnessed, this highly diffused source has the potential to satisfy all future energy needs. In the twenty-first century solar energy is expected to become increasingly attractive as an energy source because of its inexhaustible supply and its nonpolluting character, in stark contrast to the finite fossil fuels coal, petroleum, and natural gas.

CHAPTER ONE

THE SUN

Although the sun is a rather ordinary star, it is very important to the inhabitants of Earth. It is the source of virtually all Earth's energy. It provides the heat and light that make life on Earth possible. Yet Earth receives only about half a billionth of the energy that leaves the sun. The sun is a huge ball of hot gases. Like other stars, it produces enormous amounts of energy by converting hydrogen to helium deep within its interior.

The sun looks like a burning sphere. It is too hot, however, for an Earth-type chemical reaction such as burning to occur there. Besides, if burning produced its energy, it would have run out of fuel long ago. Instead, thermonuclear reactions are the source of solar energy. The vast amount of matter in the sun

The sun is a yellow dwarf star, a kind that is common in the Milky Way Galaxy. Its diameter is about 864,950 miles (1,392,000 kilometers), which is about 109 times the diameter of Earth.

can provide the "fuel" for billions of years of atomic reactions. Astronomers believe that the sun is nearly halfway through its "lifetime" of 10 billion years.

STRUCTURE AND ENERGY PRODUCTION

The sun can be divided into several different layers. Energy is produced in the dense, hot central

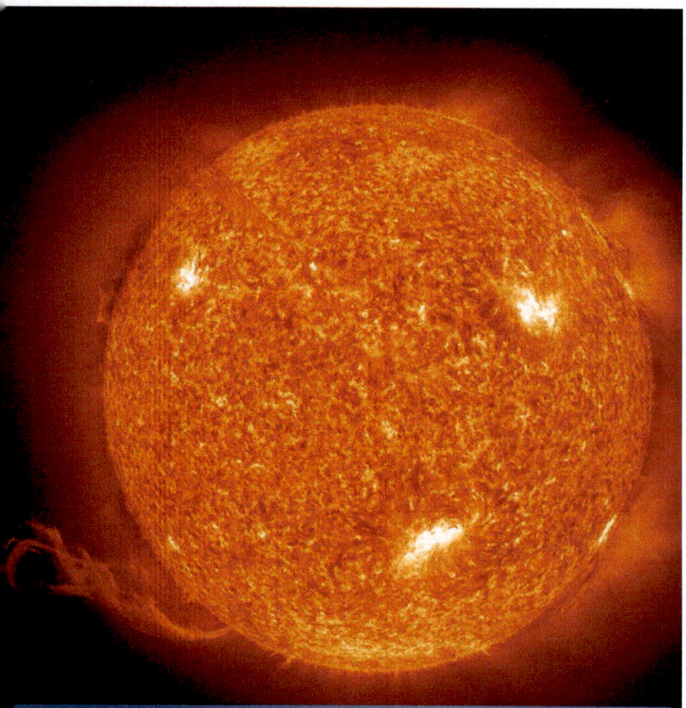

The sun is too hot for matter to exist there as a solid or liquid. Its matter consists of gas and plasma, a state in which gases are so hot that the electrons are stripped away from their atomic nuclei.

region, which is called the core, and travels outward through the rest of the interior. The surface, or the part of the sun that is visible from Earth in ordinary light, is called the photosphere. It emits most of the light and heat that reach Earth. The surface is the innermost part of the solar atmosphere. The atmosphere also has a thin middle layer, called the chromosphere, and a large outer layer, the corona. The corona gives rise to a flow of charged particles called the solar wind that stretches beyond Earth and the other planets.

The sun's core is an extremely hot, dense mass of atomic nuclei and electrons. Its temperature is about

27,000,000°F (15,000,000 Kelvin), and it is thought to be some 150 times as dense as water. The pressure is enormous. Normally, protons in atomic nuclei repel each other because they have the same electrical charge. Under the great density and pressure in the sun's core, however, nuclei can collide and fuse into new and heavier nuclei. This is a type of thermonuclear reaction called a fusion reaction.

The basic fusion process in the sun involves a series of reactions in which four hydrogen nuclei are ultimately converted into one helium nucleus. The mass of the helium nucleus is about 0.7 percent less than that of the four hydrogen nuclei. This 0.7 percent of the mass is changed into energy. Every second the sun converts almost 700 million tons (635 million metric tons) of hydrogen into about 695 million tons (630 million metric tons) of helium. Nearly 5 million tons (5 million metric tons) of mass—0.7 percent of 700 million tons (630 million metric tons)—are converted to energy. Some of this energy heats the plasma in the core and some escapes into space as nearly massless, electrically neutral particles called neutrinos. Some of the energy is in the form of gamma-ray photons. These photons travel outward from the core through a zone in which the energy is carried mainly by

Types of Electromagnetic Radiation

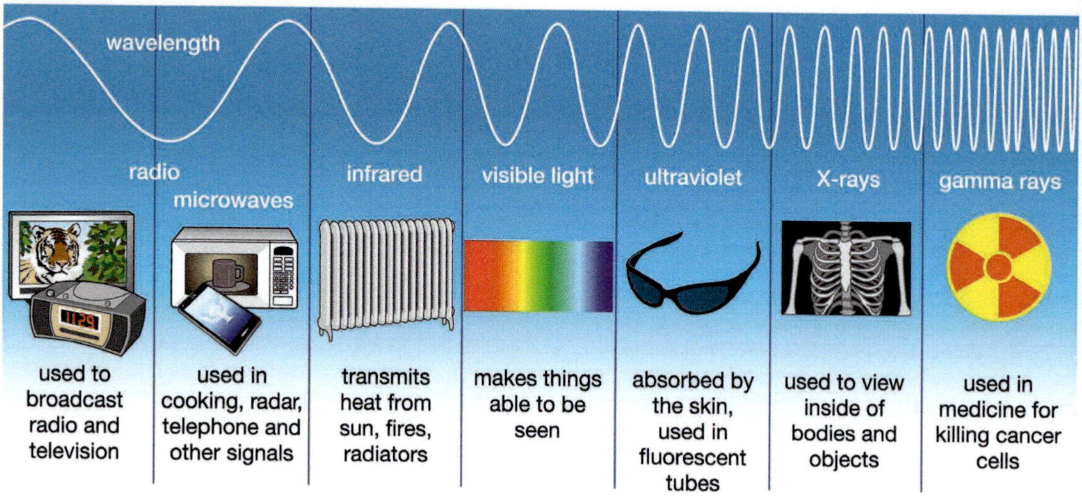

© 2013 Encyclopædia Britannica, Inc.

Radio waves, infrared rays, visible light, ultraviolet rays, X-rays, and gamma rays are all electromagnetic radiation. Radio waves have the longest wavelength, and gamma rays have the shortest wavelength.

radiation. Ultimately, the energy is emitted at the surface in many different wavelengths.

SUNLIGHT

Ordinarily, sunlight is broken down into three major components: (1) visible light, with wavelengths between 0.4 and 0.8 micrometer, (2) ultraviolet light, with wavelengths shorter than 0.4 micrometer,

ELECTROMAGNETIC RADIATION

Radiation is the movement of energy from one place to another. Electromagnetic (EM) radiation is sometimes referred to as light or radiant energy. It can travel through a vacuum as easily as it can through air and often passes through materials, such as glass, that are thought of as solid.

Light is one type of electromagnetic radiation. It is the only form of electromagnetic radiation that is visible to the naked eye. Some other kinds of electromagnetic radiation include X-rays, radio waves, and microwaves. Radiant energy travels in waves. It is caused by accelerated electric charges or by electric or magnetic fields that increase or decrease with time.

and (3) infrared radiation, with wavelengths longer than 0.8 micrometer. The visible portion constitutes nearly half of the total radiation received at the surface of Earth. Although ultraviolet light constitutes only a very small proportion of the total radiation, this component is extremely important. It produces vitamin D through the activation of ergosterol. Unfortunately, the polluted atmosphere over large

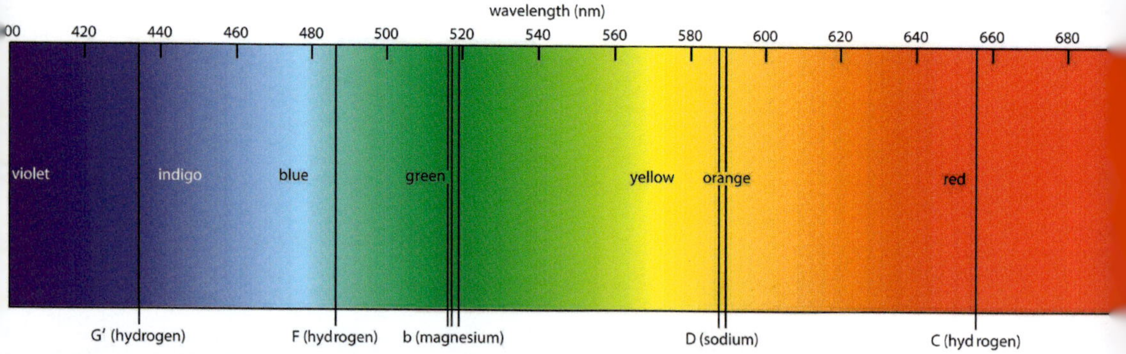

A spectrum of visible light from the sun includes prominent Fraunhofer absorption lines, representing wavelengths at which light is absorbed by particular elements.

cities robs solar radiation of a significant portion of its ultraviolet light. Infrared radiation has its chief merit in its heat-producing quality. Close to half of total solar radiation received at the surface of Earth is infrared.

CHAPTER TWO

SOLAR ENERGY COLLECTION AND CONVERSION

Some methods of solar energy collection make use of the sun's heat, while others use its light. The main types of devices used to capture solar energy and convert it to thermal energy are flat-plate collectors and concentrating collectors. Photovoltaic cells rely on the photovoltaic effect—a process in which two dissimilar materials in close contact produce an electrical voltage when struck by light or other radiant energy.

CONCENTRATING COLLECTORS

When high temperatures are needed, a concentrating, or focusing, collector is used. These devices concentrate sunlight received from a wide area onto a small, blackened receiver, thereby considerably increasing

The Noor 1 Concentrated Solar Power (CSP) plant is in Morocco. The plant uses parabolic troughs to collect sunlight. This is one of several types of concentrating collectors.

the light's intensity in order to produce high temperatures. The arrays of carefully aligned mirrors or lenses used in these so-called solar furnaces can focus enough sunlight to heat a target to temperatures of 3,600°F (2,000°C) or more. This heat can be used to study the properties of materials at high temperatures, or it can be used to operate a boiler, which in turn generates the steam for a steam-turbine–electric-generator power plant. The solar furnace has become an important tool in high-temperature research. For producing steam, the movable mirrors are so arranged as to concentrate large amounts of solar radiation upon blackened pipes through which water is circulated and thereby heated.

FLAT-PLATE COLLECTORS

The most common flat-plate collectors consist of a dark metal plate, covered with one or two sheets of glass, that absorbs heat. The heat is transferred to air or water, called carrier fluids, that flows past the back of the plate. Flat-plate collectors are used for home and hot-water heating. Flat-plate collectors typically heat carrier fluids to temperatures ranging from 150° to 200°F (66° to 93°C). The efficiency of such

This man is installing flat-plate solar collectors for a hot-water heating system on the roof of a house.

collectors varies from 20 to 80 percent, depending on the design of the collector.

Flat-plate collectors are employed in active solar heating systems (as opposed to passive heating, which relies on architectural design to heat buildings). In active heating, mechanical means are used to store, collect, and distribute solar energy in buildings in order to provide hot water or space heating. The sunlight falling on a building's collector array is

PASSIVE SOLAR HEATING

A building's site, structure, and materials can all be utilized to maximize the heating (and lighting) effect of the sunlight falling on it, thereby lowering or even eliminating its fuel requirement. A well-insulated building with a large glass window facing south, for instance, can effectively trap heat on sunny days and reduce reliance on gas or oil (for heating) or electricity (for lighting). Entering sunlight warms the air and the solid surfaces in those rooms exposed to it, and this warmth is carried to other rooms in the building by natural convection. Interior finishes such as brick or tile are often incorporated into buildings to absorb the sunlight and reradiate the heat at night.

converted to heat, which is transferred to a carrier fluid that is then pumped to a conversion, storage, and distribution system. In liquid-based systems, water (or less commonly glycol) is pumped through tubes that are in contact with a flat-plate collector. The collector's blackened metal plate absorbs sunlight and is insulated on the front with layers of glass and air. The glass allows visible light to fall on the plate but traps the resulting heat, which is then transferred to the carrier fluid. Alternatively, the fluid may be pumped through an evacuated glass tube or a volume of space onto which a large volume of sunlight has been focused (and hence concentrated) by reflecting mirrors.

After picking up heat from the collector, the carrier fluid is pumped down to an insulated storage tank, where it can be used immediately or stored for later use. The system can supply a home with hot water drawn from the storage tank, or, with the warmed water flowing through tubes in floors and ceilings, it can provide space heating. The storage tank allows water heated during sunny periods to be used at night or during cloudy days. If the carrier fluid contains antifreeze to keep it from freezing during cold weather, a heat exchanger is used to transfer the carrier fluid's heat to water that can

Solar farms are also known as photovoltaic power stations. They consist of huge solar-panel arrays and supply power for utilities.

be used for domestic purposes. Residential heating systems using flat-plate collectors typically heat carrier fluids to temperatures between 150° and 200°F (66° and 93°C).

Hot-air solar systems use more complex collectors that heat air directly. Because air cannot store much thermal energy, however, supplementary storage systems must be added. They consist of rock beds or assemblies of large pebbles that are heated by the air flowing through the collector. Room air then passes over the storage bed and absorbs heat from the rocks.

PHOTOVOLTAIC SYSTEMS

Solar radiation may be converted directly into electricity by photovoltaic cells, or solar cells. In such cells, a small electric voltage is generated when light strikes the junction between a metal and a semiconductor (such as silicon) or the junction between two different semiconductors. The power generated by a single photovoltaic cell is typically only about two watts. By connecting large numbers of individual cells together, however, as in solar-panel arrays, hundreds or even thousands of kilowatts of electric power can be generated in a solar electric plant.

A complete photovoltaic system may consist of many solar panels, a power system for accommodating different electrical loads, an external circuit, and storage batteries. Photovoltaic systems are broadly classifiable as either stand-alone or grid-connected systems. Stand-alone systems contain a solar array and a bank of batteries directly wired to an application or load circuit. A battery system is essential to compensate for the absence of any electrical output from the cells at night or in overcast conditions; this adds considerably to the overall cost. Each battery stores direct current (DC) electricity at a fixed voltage determined by the panel specifications, although load requirements may differ. DC-to-DC converters are used to provide the voltage levels demanded by DC loads, and DC-to-AC inverters supply power to alternating current (AC) loads. Stand-alone systems are ideally suited for remote installations where linking to a central power station is prohibitively expensive. Examples include pumping water for feedstock and providing electric power to lighthouses, telecommunications repeater stations, and mountain lodges.

Photovoltaic panels can be used both as part of vast solar farms and to provide electricity to individual houses like the one here.

Grid-connected systems integrate solar arrays with public utility power grids in two ways. One-way systems are used by utilities to supplement power grids during midday peak usage. Bidirectional systems are used by companies and individuals to supply some or all of their power needs, with any excess power fed back into a utility power grid. A major advantage of grid-connected systems is that no storage batteries are needed. The corresponding reduction in capital and maintenance costs is offset, however, by the increased complexity of the system. Inverters and additional protective gear are needed to interface low-voltage DC output from the solar array with a high-voltage AC power grid. Additionally, rate structures for reverse metering are necessary when residential and industrial solar systems feed energy back into a utility grid.

The simplest deployment of solar panels is on a tilted support frame or rack known as a fixed mount. For maximum efficiency, a fixed mount should face south in the Northern Hemisphere or north in the Southern Hemisphere, and it should have a tilt angle from horizontal of about 15 degrees less than the local latitude in summer and 25 degrees more than the local latitude in winter. More complicated deployments involve motor-driven tracking systems

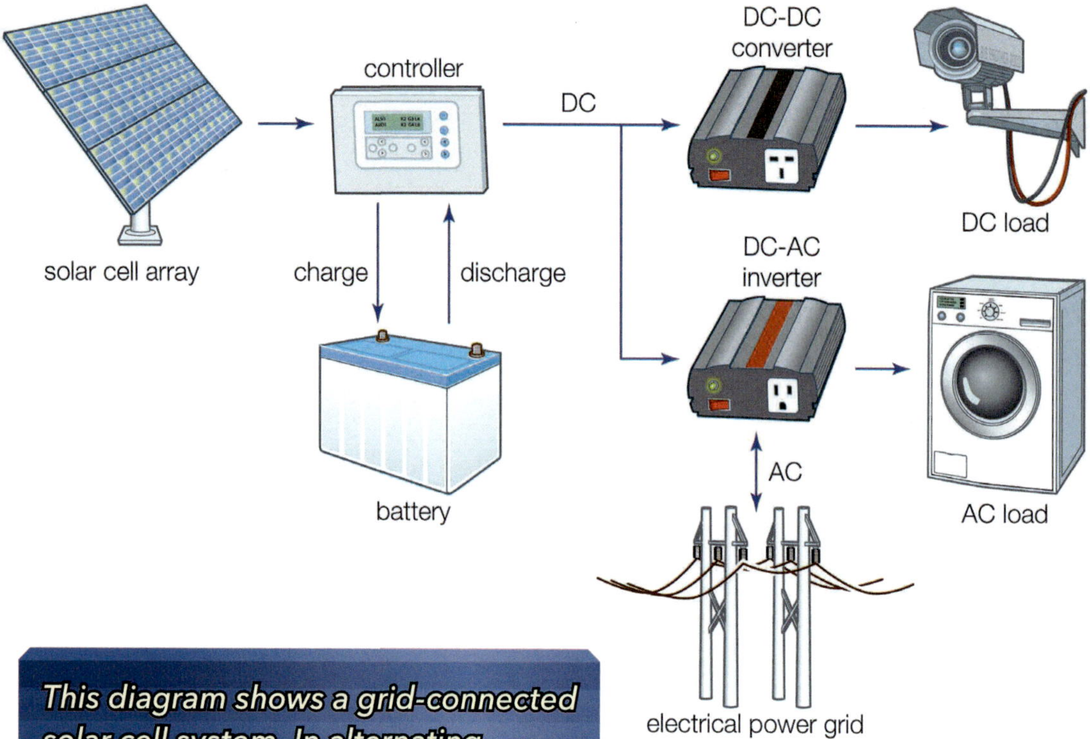

This diagram shows a grid-connected solar cell system. In alternating current the motion of the electric charges is periodically reversed; in direct current it is not.

that continually reorient the panels to follow the daily and seasonal movements of the sun. Such systems are justified only for large-scale utility generation using high-efficiency concentrator solar cells with lenses or parabolic mirrors that can intensify solar radiation a hundredfold or more.

Solar energy can be collected only when the sun shines. That makes storage an important aspect of many solar systems.

STORAGE

Solar-energy collection is variable and does not necessarily match the changing demand for energy. Consequently, some form of energy storage is necessary to save energy for use during times when there is little or no sunlight. The electrical power from photovoltaic cells can be stored in electric storage batteries. In systems that use the collected energy to heat a fluid, the fluid may be directly stored in an insulated tank or the energy may be transferred to another storage medium, such as a bed of rocks.

CHAPTER THREE

SOLAR CELLS

A solar cell is any device that directly converts the energy of light into electrical energy through the photovoltaic effect. The overwhelming majority of solar cells are made from silicon.

Solar cells can be arranged into large groupings called arrays. These arrays, composed of many thousands of individual cells, can function as central electric power stations, converting sunlight into electrical energy for distribution to industrial, commercial, and residential users. Solar cells in much smaller configurations, commonly referred to as solar cell panels or simply solar panels, have been installed by homeowners on their rooftops to replace or augment their conventional electric supply. Because they have no moving parts that could need maintenance or fuels that would require replenishment, solar cells provide power for most space installations, from communications and weather satellites to space stations. (Solar power is insufficient for space probes sent to the outer planets of the solar system or into interstellar space, however, because of the diffusion of radiant energy with distance from the sun.) Solar cells have also been used in consumer products, such as electronic toys, handheld calculators, and portable radios. Solar cells used in devices of this kind may utilize artificial light (for example, from incandescent and fluorescent lamps) as well as sunlight.

Space stations use large panels of solar cells and banks of storage batteries as their source of electrical power.

SOLAR CELL STRUCTURE AND OPERATION

All solar cells have the same basic structure. Light enters the device through an optical coating, or antireflection layer, that minimizes the loss of light by reflection. It effectively traps the light falling on the solar cell by promoting its transmission to the energy-conversion layers below. The antireflection layer is typically an oxide of silicon, tantalum, or titanium.

The three energy-conversion layers below the antireflection layer are the top junction layer, absorber layer (which constitutes the core of the device), and the back junction layer. Two additional electrical contact layers are needed to carry the electric current out to an external load and back into the cell, thus completing an electric circuit. The electrical contact layer on the face of the cell where light enters is generally present in some grid pattern and is composed of a good conductor such as a metal. Since metal blocks light, the grid lines are as thin and widely spaced as is possible without impairing collection of the current produced by the cell. The back electrical contact layer has no such restrictions. It need simply function as an electrical contact and thus covers the entire back

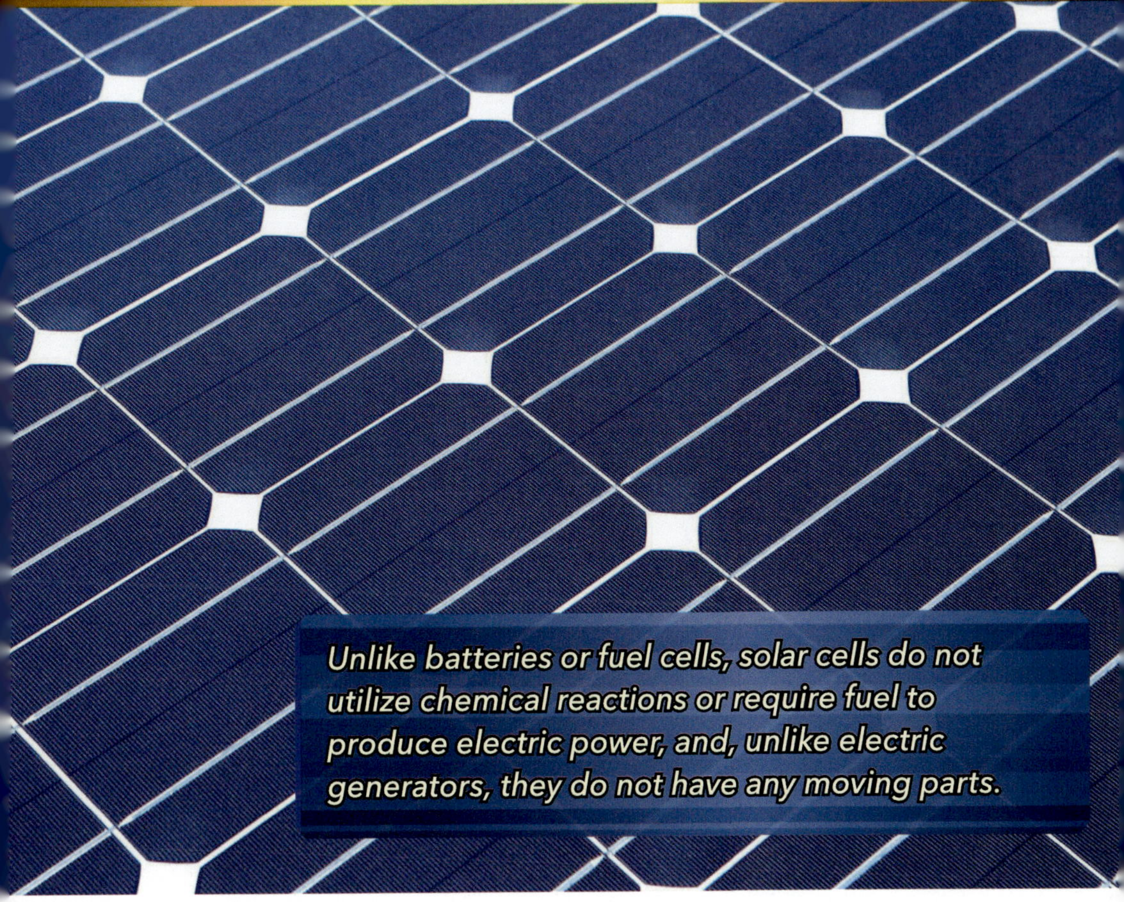

Unlike batteries or fuel cells, solar cells do not utilize chemical reactions or require fuel to produce electric power, and, unlike electric generators, they do not have any moving parts.

surface of the cell structure. Because the back layer also must be a very good electrical conductor, it is always made of metal.

Since most of the energy in sunlight and artificial light is in the visible range of electromagnetic radiation, a solar cell absorber should be efficient in absorbing radiation at those wavelengths. Materials that strongly absorb visible radiation belong to a class of substances known as semiconductors.

SEMICONDUCTORS

Used to make various kinds of electronic devices, semiconductors are a class of solids that have an ability to conduct electricity between that of a conductor and that of an insulator. Semiconductors in thicknesses of about 0.004 inches (0.01 centimeters) or less can absorb all incident visible light. Since the junction-forming and contact layers are much thinner, the thickness of a solar cell is essentially that of the absorber. Examples of semiconductor materials employed in solar cells include silicon, gallium arsenide, indium phosphide, and copper indium selenide.

When light falls on a solar cell, electrons in the absorber layer are excited from a lower-energy "ground state," in which they are bound to specific atoms in the solid, to a higher "excited state," in which they can move through the solid. In the absence of the junction-forming layers, these "free" electrons are in random motion, and so there can be no oriented direct current. The addition of junction-forming layers, however, induces a built-in electric field that produces the photovoltaic effect. In effect, the electric field gives a collective motion

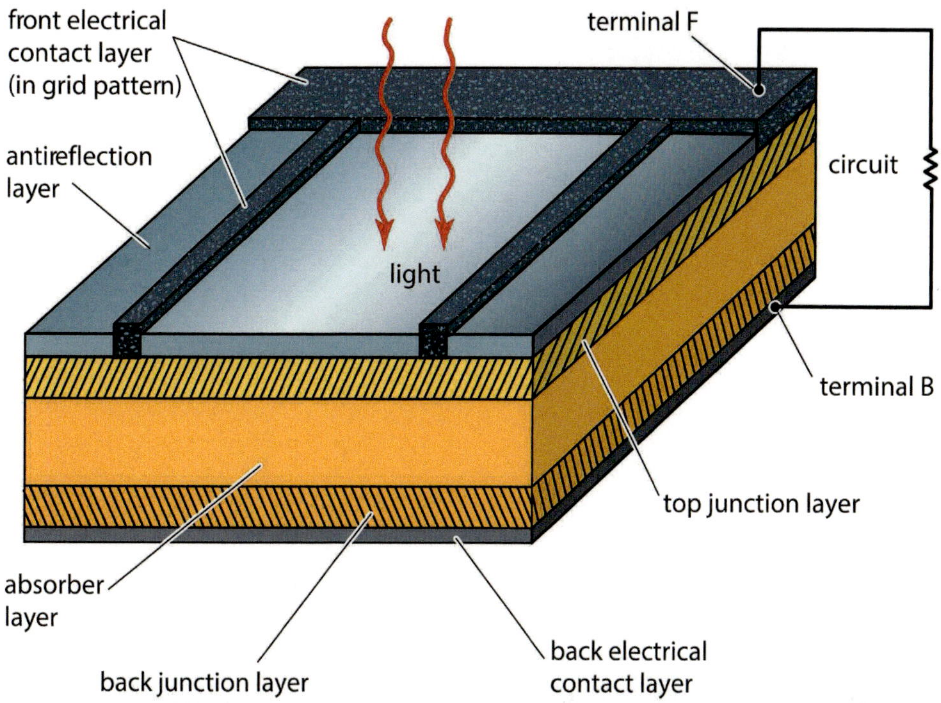

This diagram shows a commonly used solar cell structure. In many such cells, the absorber layer and the back junction layer are both made of the same material.

to the electrons that flow past the electrical contact layers into an external circuit where they can do useful work.

The materials used for the two junction-forming layers must be dissimilar to the absorber in order to produce the built-in electric field and to carry the electric current. Hence, these may be different semiconductors (or the same semiconductor with different types of conduction), or they may be a metal and a semiconductor.

The photovoltaic process bears certain similarities to photosynthesis, the process by which the energy in light is converted into chemical energy in plants. Since solar cells obviously cannot produce electric power in the dark, part of the energy they develop under light is stored, in many applications, for use when light is not available. One common means of storing this electrical energy is by charging electrochemical storage batteries. This sequence of converting the energy in light into the energy of excited electrons and then into stored chemical energy is strikingly similar to the process of photosynthesis.

SOLAR PANEL DESIGN

Most solar cells are small and protected from the environment by a thin coating of glass or transparent plastic. Because a typical 4 inch × 4 inch (10 cm × 10 cm) solar cell generates only about two watts of electrical power (15 to 20 percent of the energy of light incident on their surface), cells are usually combined in series to boost the voltage or in parallel to increase the current. A solar, or photovoltaic, module generally consists of thirty-six interconnected cells laminated to glass within an aluminum frame. In turn, one or more of these modules may be wired and framed together to form a solar panel. Solar panels are slightly less efficient at energy conversion per surface area than individual cells, because of inevitable inactive areas in the assembly and cell-to-cell variations in performance. The back of each solar panel is equipped with standardized sockets so that its output can be combined with other solar panels to form a solar array.

This worker is installing solar modules, or panels. Together, the modules make up a solar array. Modules themselves are made up of several solar cells.

use of fossil fuels in industry, transportation, and construction has added large amounts of CO_2 to Earth's atmosphere. CO_2 behaves as a greenhouse gas—that is, it absorbs infrared radiation (net heat energy) emitted from Earth's surface and reradiates it back to the surface. Thus, the substantial CO_2 increase in the atmosphere is a major contributing factor to human-induced global warming.

THE DRAWBACKS OF SOLAR ENERGY

Though solar energy itself is free, the high cost of its collection, conversion, and storage limits its exploitation. According to the U.S. Energy Information Administration, solar energy accounted for just 1.3 percent of the electricity generated at utility-scale facilities in the United States in 2017. The World Energy Council's 2016 World Energy Resources report notes that solar energy produced 1 percent of the electricity used worldwide in 2015.

The cost of materials and available space must be considered in designing a solar system. Less-efficient solar panels imply more panels, occupying more space, in order to produce the same amount of electricity. The energy efficiency of most

This massive solar farm is located in Webberville, Texas. While solar farms provide clean, renewable energy, solar power remains an expensive option.

present-day photovoltaic cells is only about 15 to 20 percent, and since the intensity of solar radiation is low to begin with, huge and costly assemblies of such cells are required to produce even moderate amounts of power.

There are issues with solar thermal power as well. Thermal solar power systems in homes provide heat and hot water, but not electricity. They require maintenance and when something goes wrong—such as if the water in a liquid-based system freezes—it can be disastrous.

SPECIAL CONSIDERATIONS FOR SPACE

Compromises between cost of materials and efficiency are particularly evident for space-based solar systems. Panels used on satellites have to be extra-rugged, reliable, and resistant to radiation damage encountered in Earth's upper atmosphere. In addition, minimizing the liftoff weight of these panels is more critical than fabrication costs. Another factor in solar panel design is the ability to fabricate cells in "thin-film" form on a variety of substrates, such as glass, ceramic, and plastic, for more flexible deployment. Amorphous silicon is very attractive from this viewpoint. In particular, amorphous silicon-coated roof tiles and other photovoltaic materials have been introduced in architectural design and for recreational vehicles, boats, and automobiles.

Another limitation is that solar energy can only be collected during daylight hours—and only when the weather is sufficiently sunny. The amount of sunlight is dependent on the extent of the daytime cloud cover. Some places on Earth receive more than 4,000 hours per year of sunlight (more than 90 percent of

This solar farm is in Rosamond, California, near the Mojave Desert. Deserts are a good location for solar energy, as they get a lot of sun.

the maximum possible), as in the Sahara. Others receive less than 2,000 hours, as in regions of frequent storminess, such as Scotland and Iceland. This makes certain parts of the world—Northern Europe, for instance—less than ideal candidates for solar power. While improvements to the global power grid would make this less of an obstacle, such updates are slow and expensive.

SOLAR ENERGY'S POTENTIAL

The potential for solar energy is enormous. Each day the Earth receives in the form of solar energy about 200,000 times the total world electrical-generating capacity. Researchers are experimenting with solar power in a variety of contexts.

One scheme that has been proposed for the future is the use of satellite solar-power stations to supply

The sun is the source of almost all energy on Earth. Thanks to new technologies, we now have ways to capture solar energy more directly.

power to Earth. In this scheme, a satellite equipped with large solar panels would collect solar energy constantly, bypassing atmospheric interference. The electricity would be converted to microwaves and then beamed to Earth, where the microwave energy would be converted back to electricity for distribution.

Calculations based on the world's projected energy consumption by 2030 suggest that global energy demands would be fulfilled by solar panels operating at 20 percent efficiency and covering only about 191,817 square miles (496,805 square km) of Earth's surface. The material requirements would be enormous but feasible, as silicon is the second most abundant element in Earth's crust. These factors have led solar proponents to envision a future "solar economy" in which practically all of humanity's energy requirements are satisfied by cheap, clean, renewable sunlight.

GLOSSARY

ATOMIC Relating to atoms, the tiny particles that are the basic building blocks of all matter.

CHEMICAL REACTION A process in which one or more substances are converted to one or more different substances.

CIRCUIT The complete path of an electric current.

CONVECTION A process through which heat is transferred by the movement of a heated fluid.

ELECTRON An elementary particle that has a negative charge and travels around the nucleus of an atom.

ERGOSTEROL A steroid that is converted by ultraviolet irradiation into ergocalciferol (vitamin D2), which promotes proper bone development in mammals.

FLUID A substance tending to flow or take the shape of its container. Liquids and gases are fluids.

FUSION The union of light atomic nuclei to form heavier nuclei resulting in the release of enormous quantities of energy.

GENERATOR A machine by which mechanical energy is changed into electrical energy.

LATITUDE The distance north or south from the equator, as measured in degrees.

NUCLEUS (plural **NUCLEI**) The central part of an atom that consists of protons and usually neutrons.

PARABOLIC Bowl-shaped.

PHOTON A tiny particle or bundle of electromagnetic radiation.

PHOTOSYNTHESIS A process by which plants, algae, and certain microorganisms transform light energy from the sun into the chemical energy of food.

PLASMA A collection of charged particles that shows some characteristics of a gas but that differs from a gas in being a good conductor of electricity and in being affected by a magnetic field.

POWER GRID A network of electrical transmission lines connecting a multiplicity of generating stations to loads over a wide area.

PROTON An atomic particle that occurs in the nucleus of every atom and carries a positive charge equal in size to the negative charge of an electron.

RADIATION The process of giving off radiant energy in the form of waves or particles.

THERMONUCLEAR Of or relating to the transformations in the nucleus of atoms of low atomic weight (as hydrogen) that require a very high temperature.

TURBINE An engine whose central driving shaft is fitted with a series of blades spun around by the pressure of a fluid (as water, steam, or air).

UTILITY A business providing a public service (as power or water).

VOLTAGE A measurement of electric potential.

FOR MORE INFORMATION

Bethea, Nikole Brooks. *Power Plays: The Next 100 Years of Energy*. Mankato, MN: Capstone Press, 2017.

Bow, James. *Energy from the Sun: Solar Power* (Next Generation Energy). New York, NY: Crabtree Publishing Company, 2016.

Bright, Michael. *From Sunshine to Light Bulb*. New York, NY: Crabtree Publishing Company, 2017.

Conley, Kate A. *Solar Energy* (Core Library: Alternative Energy) Minneapolis, MN: ABDO Publishing, 2017.

Dickmann, Nancy. *Harnessing Solar Energy* (The Future of Power). New York, NY: PowerKids Press, 2017.

Doeden, Matt. *Finding Out About Solar Energy* (Searchlight Books: What Are Energy Sources?). Minneapolis, MN: Lerner Publications Company, 2015.

Grady, Colin. *Solar Energy* (Saving the Planet through Green Energy). New York, NY: Enslow Publishing, 2017.

Hardyman, Robyn. *How a Solar-Powered Home Works* (Eco Works). New York, NY: Gareth Stevens Publishing, 2014.

Kallen, Stuart A. *Real-World STEM: Develop Economical Solar Power.* (San Diego, CA: ReferencePoint Press, Inc., 2018.

Kenney, Karen Latchana. *Energy Investigations* (Alternator Books: Key Questions in Physical Science). Minneapolis, MN: Lerner Publications, 2018.

Mason, Helen. *Energy Entrepreneurs* (Science and Technology Start-Up Stars). New York, NY: Crabtree Publishing Company, 2018.

Otfinoski, Steven. *Wind, Solar, and Geothermal Power: From Concept to Consumer.* New York, NY: Children's Press, 2016.

Ringstad, Arnold. *The Science of Solar Energy* (Size of Renewable Energy). San Diego, CA: ReferencePoint Press, Inc., 2018.

Scibilia, Jade Zora. *Solar Panels: Harnessing the Power of the Sun* (Powered Up! A STEM Approach to Energy Sources). New York, NY: PowerKids Press, 2018.

Small, Cathleen. *Wind, Waves, and the Sun: The Rise of Alternative Energy* (The History of Conservation: Preserving Our Planet) New York, NY: Cavendish Square Publishing, 2018.

Sullivan, Laura L. *The Pros and Cons of Solar Power* (The Economics of Energy). New York, NY: Cavendish Square Publishing, 2015.

WEBSITES

International Energy Agency
https://www.iea.org/topics/renewables/solar/
Facebook: @internationalenergyagency; Twitter: @IEA

National Renewable Energy Laboratory
https://www.nrel.gov/workingwithus/re-solar.html
Facebook: @nationalrenewableenergylab;
Twitter: @nrel

Solar Energy Industries Association (SEIA)
https://www.seia.org/initiatives/about-solar-energy
Facebook, YouTube: @TheSolarIndustry;
Twitter: @SEIA

U.S. Department of Energy
https://energy.gov/science-innovation/energy-sources/renewable-energy/solar
Facebook: @energygov; Instagram, Twitter: @energy

INDEX